THE ANGEL'S DICTIONARY

A SPIRITED GLOSSARY FOR THE LITTLE DEVIL IN YOU

ALSO BY SOL LUCKMAN

FICTION

Snooze: A Story of Awakening

NONFICTION

Conscious Healing

Potentiate Your DNA

For myself, mostly

All are lunatics, but he who can analyze his delusion is called a philosopher.

—Ambrose Bierce

The Angel's Dictionary

Introduction

Of all the anthologized American literature I devoured in my high school English classes, none stuck in my mind quite like, or quite as long as, Ambrose Bierce's wickedly satirical masterpiece, *The Devil's Dictionary*.

Putting aside any pretense to conformity or prudishness on my part, I'm the first to admit this deliciously warped glossary—originally titled *The Cynic's Word Book* when it appeared in 1906—appealed primarily to the little devil in my wayward teenage self.

A master wordsmith in the comical vein of his good buddy Mark Twain (whom he uncannily resembled and to whom he is often compared), Bierce indelibly defined *love* as "a temporary insanity curable by marriage," *litigation* as "a machine which you go into as a pig and come out of as a sausage," *patience* as "a minor form of despair, disguised as a virtue," and an *egotist* as "a person of low taste, more interested in himself than in me."

If you don't find these definitions hilarious, or at least amusing, I advise you to stop reading now and go rustle up a sense of humor before it's too late.

While studying literature in college and trying my hand at fiction, I developed a habit of keeping writing journals inspired by *The Notebooks of F. Scott Fitzgerald* in which I jotted down everything from jokes and snippets of dialogue to plotlines and ideas for character development.

It may come as a surprise to readers with a lingering impression of the gravitas of Fitzgerald's rather serious novels that some of his private humor—epigrammatic and devoid of context—recalled Bierce. "Thank gravity for working your bowels," quipped Fitzgerald, who also wittily observed, "There are no second acts in American lives."

In my opinion, Fitzgerald's most gut-busting notebook entry came in the form of his famous Turkey Recipes, a series of farcical "cocktail tall tales" with a tongue-in-cheek cookbook delivery that included my favorite "definition" ...

Turkey with Whiskey Sauce: This recipe is for a party of four. Obtain a gallon of whiskey, and allow it to age for several hours. Then serve, allowing one quart for each guest. The next day the turkey should be added, little by little, constantly stirring and basting.

One recurring category in my own notebooks—no surprise here—has been satirical definitions. For many years I thought I was merely scribbling these bite-sized bursts of irreverence for my eyes only in a private homage to the Biercean and Fitzgeraldean spirit of subversion.

And maybe I was. But that changed last year when, for one reason or another, whole new crops of snarky definitions started sprouting up in my cerebral cortex as I found myself feverishly assembling *The Angel's Dictionary*, if only for my own satisfaction.

You might be inclined to jump right in and start reading the entries. That's okay—that's why I put them there. But if you're interested in hearing my perspective on this *Spirited Glossary for the Little Devil in You*, stick with me.

You see, the biggest conundrum with publishing a book of satire isn't the risk that no one will laugh at your jokes (some of which, admittedly, fall into the hopelessly adolescent category); the most troubling issue—for the satirist anyway—is the sad likelihood that hardly anyone will even feel *insulted* by them.

As it turns out, the critical flaw with any attempt at satire may be baked into the genre. Most dictionaries define satire in something like these terms: *a work of literature in which human ignorance, immorality and hypocrisy are exposed through wit, irony, sarcasm, burlesque, exaggeration, or ridicule.*

I'm fine with that definition. But it doesn't tell you whether satire is actually capable of *changing* anything.

Satire's Golden Age—in English literature at least—was the 18th century. During this sublimely sardonic literary period, the effectiveness of the satirical mode was appraised from antithetical perspectives by two irreverent geniuses with just the right temperament to perfect the art.

Henry Fielding, author of the epically picaresque *Tom Jones*, wrote, "The satirist is to be regarded as our physician, not our enemy." Taking a more pessimistic view, Jonathan Swift of *Gulliver's Travels* fame defined satire as "a sort of glass, wherein beholders do generally discover everybody's face but their own; which is the chief reason for that kind of reception it meets in the world, and that so very few are offended with it."

Brushing aside any Fieldingesque idealization of satire as social medicine, a jocund pill capable of magically curing the satirized of their thickheadedness and ethical lapses, Swift paints the genre as an innocuous method of sermonizing. According to this jaded perspective, readers can stare until they're blue in the face into the mirror of satire—but the warped surface undulates like a carnival mirror and, in most cases, they don't even manage to recognize themselves.

Across the big pond a century and a half later in *The Devil's Dictionary*, Bierce defined satire, well, *satirically*. He took particular aim at his fellow Americans:

> *SATIRE: n. An obsolete kind of literary composition in which the vices and follies of the author's enemies were expounded with imperfect tenderness. In this country satire never had more than a sickly and uncertain existence, for the soul of it is wit, wherein we are dolefully deficient, the humor that we mistake for it, like all humor, being tolerant and sympathetic. Moreover, although Americans are "endowed by their Creator" with abundant vice and folly, it is not generally known that these are reprehensible qualities, wherefore the satirist is popularly regarded as a soul-spirited knave, and his ever victim's outcry for codefendants evokes a national assent.*

Even though history remembers him as one of America's most gifted satirists, Bierce unflinchingly represents satire as a thing of the past, a relic woefully unsuited to the sappy American sense of humor of his day. Simultaneously, the satirist is depicted as an idealistic fool swimming against the current of accepted vice and folly, his message falling on deaf ears and rendering him, effectively, a satirical victim of his own art.

So, where precisely does yours truly register on the Fielding-Swift-Bierce satirical scale? Does the author of *The Angel's Dictionary* intend to heal a mad world, if only a little, by good-naturedly mocking it? Does he—smug in his "sane" role as satirist—merely stick his tongue out at humanity's insanity as if to sneer, "I told you so"? Or is he really just another "lunatic," to reference this book's epigraph, "who can analyze his delusion"?

The answer, to be a good deal more transparent than any administration in recent history, is maybe a little of all three.

One point I won't waffle on is this: I learned in composing this dictionary that I'm *not* Ambrose Bierce. By which I mean: I may or may not be as witty an aphorist, but I'm unquestionably not as great a *cynic*, defined herein as "one who gets off the train before it reaches the station." Thus while Bierce justly deserved the epithet "Bitter Bierce," I titled my latter-day compendium of social inanity angelically first—and only secondarily devilish.

With or without satire, though just maybe a tiny bit faster with it, when all is said and done, I believe we humans will pull through and—despite ourselves—get the world right one of these days.

Sol Luckman

December 2016

A SPIRITED GLOSSARY FOR THE LITTLE DEVIL IN YOU

Tip #1: Read each entry carefully to raise your awareness of reality or, at least, not lower it.

Tip #2: To supplement this glossary for your closet satire junkie, visit www.CrowRising.com and sign up to receive the author's Devilishly Clever Word of the Day free in your inbox.

abhorigine: (n.) member of any decimated indigenous culture with darn good reason to hate the White Man.

academia: (n.) terminal condition in which the head gradually swells while the heart slowly atrophies.

The cards are stacked (quite properly, I imagine) against all professional aesthetes, and no doubt we all deserve the dark, wordy, academic deaths we all sooner or later die. —J.D. Salinger

accomplishmint: (n.) breath mint that makes one feel proud.

acne: (n.) upper limit just above the tan line where zits can form peaks on the human body.

activism: (n.) opting for a lifestyle of getting off your ass.

alien invasion: (n.) apparently, judging by the motion picture industry's obsessive-compulsive fixation on the subject, what Hollywood is conditioning the public to buy into.

allopathic medicine: (n.) celebrated newfangled method of dissecting a whole spiritual person into material bits and pieces, treating symptoms without regard to their emotional and energetic causation, routinely misdiagnosing patients, and prescribing unnecessary drugs and surgeries (thanks to lucrative kickbacks) that often result in death or, worse, wishing you were dead.

Take two vaccines and call me in the morning. —Yours Truly

al-Qaeda: (n.) CIA in Arabic.

altercation: (n.) fashion conflict with a belligerent seamstress.

America: (n.) not what it used to be.

American Dream: (n.) it started out all peaches and cream, but unfortunately degenerated into a nightmare.

We have two American flags always: one for the rich and one for the poor. —*Henry Miller*

American-owned: (adj.) archaic for Chinese-owned.

anarchy: (n.) radical social experiment about which everyone seems to have a knee-jerk opinion but which no one has ever put to the test.

I think people should be allowed to do anything they want. We haven't tried that for a while. Maybe this time it'll work. —*George Carlin*

ancient alien: (n.) extraterrestrial who is extremely old.

androgynous: (n.) ambiguously erogenous.

android: (n.) modern male glued to a cell phone.

angel: (n.) one who gets a kick out of not having fun.

Angels can fly because they take themselves lightly.
—G.K. Chesterton

anthropology: (n.) academic discipline institutionally designed to obscure and distort the true story of human origins.

antibiotic: (n.) drug that requires immediate administration of probiotics.

antidepressant: (n.) any of various energetic techniques for warding off parasitic friends, colleagues, and family members.

antivaxxer: (n.) prolifer.

Vaccination is a barbarous practice and one of the most fatal of all the delusions current in our time. —Mahatma Gandhi

apologist: (n.) one who is paid to be sorry.

Talking is where we go wrong. —Yours Truly

appathy: (n.) emotional burnout resulting from overexposure to unnecessary software.

archeogastronomy: (n.) science devoted to the study of foods from other star systems.

Archon: (n.) ancient Gnostic term for any asswipe control freak who abuses power—on or off the planet.

artificial intelligence (AI): (n.) transhumanist substitute for genuine intelligence.

asbestos: (n.) FDA-proposed carcinogenic material for dinnerware to go with EPA-approved household light bulbs brimming with neurotoxic mercury.

ascension: (n.) levitating from meditating.

Be here now. —Ram Dass

asstrollogy: (n.) study of how the stars foretell the ways in which paid Internet trolls make asses of themselves.

astroturfing: (n.) walking uninvited all over someone else's star.

atheist: (n.) one who dislikes people who believe in God.

The first gulp from the glass of natural sciences will turn you into an atheist, but at the bottom of the glass God is waiting for you.
—Werner Heisenberg

Atlantis: (n.) new-agey suburb of Atlanta, Georgia.

attachment parenting: (n.) big improvement on detachment parenting.

attention deficit disorder (ADD): (n.) fabricated diagnosis to turn those who are simply youthful and curious into automatons while drug companies and the doctors who pimp their wares profit.

attorney: (n.) career conman with a fancy office.

aural sex: (n.) erotic kisses to the energy body.

autism: (n.) freeze response of a young mind when a tiny body is subjected to the horrors of modern medicine.

awakening: (n.) experience of opening one's eyes to the way the world is not.

I am not a teacher, but an awakener. —Robert Frost

baby boomer: (n.) member of the first me-first generation.

bad news: (n.) any news reported by mainstream or alternative media.

Certainly it constitutes bad news when the people who agree with you are buggier than batshit. —Philip K. Dick

bad sex: (n.) no such phenomenon has yet to be observed by biologists.

bag lady: (n.) wealthy woman who, in designer purse purchases alone, spends enough money to feed the homeless.

bait and switch: (n.) Facebook's game-changing marketing plan.

banana republic: (n.) lawless society where the monkeys rule.

banker: (n.) scam of the earth.

A banker is a fellow who lends you his umbrella when the sun is shining, but wants it back the minute it begins to rain.
—Mark Twain

banking system: (n.) money mafia dangling governments from corporate strings.

bankrupt: (v. or adj.) term describing the explosion of an insolvent bank.

banned book: (n.) required reading.

If you absolutely must flaunt your faults for posterity, publish a book. —Yours Truly

barbitchirate: (n.) prickly, enraged feminist on downers.

baseball fan: (n.) swing and a miss.

basturd: (n.) stool born out of wedlock.

bathroom: (n.) where Americans go to argue about gender while the country goes down the toilet.

bedsore: (adj.) describes the haggard sensation of having slept around too much.

beggar: (n.) formerly, member of the middle class.

belly dance: (n.) cellulite jiggle of the McDonald's crowd.

benign tumor: (n.) former US president lacking power to further harm the body politic.

bigamist: (n.) one who prefers large wives.

Big Bang: (n.) never happened.

We are asked by science to believe that the entire universe sprang from nothingness, and at a single point and for no discernible reason. This notion is the limit case for credulity. In other words, if you can believe this, you can believe anything. —Terrence McKenna

Big Brother: (n.) Uncle Sam's private persona.

Bilderberg Club: (n.) yearly Illuminati think tank for world domination where theories become conspiracies.

Bill of Rights: (n.) official tally of how much our rights cost to keep.

Everything is backwards; everything is upside down. Doctors destroy health, lawyers destroy justice, universities destroy knowledge, governments destroy freedom, the major media destroy information and religions destroy spirituality. —Michael Ellner

birth control: (n.) much easier said than done.

birther: (n.) anyone who demands proof that the president was born as opposed to hatched.

*An idea that is not dangerous is not worthy of being called an idea
at all.* —Oscar Wilde

bitch slap: (n.) handler's backhand to the head of a corrupt presidential candidate that makes her "short-circuit."

blanket statement: (n.) observation stenciled on an American quilt used to cover up inconvenient truths.

blowjob: (n.) State of the Union address.

blue genes: (n.) inherited predisposition to unhappiness.

bombast: (n.) boasting of war crimes.

bombshell: (n.) click-bait term employed in alternative news titles that usually signals overblown content of no real revolutionary import.

boob job: (n.) apt description of the average administration.

brain fart: (n.) noxious gas emitted when mainstream journalists commit their thoughts to paper.

> *I tell you, we are here on Earth to fart around, and don't let anybody tell you different. —Kurt Vonnegut*

brain fog: (n.) state of perpetual fuzzy-headedness in the public resulting from weather modification via chemtrails.

brain wave: (n.) act of mentally saying hello.

Brazil: (n.) famed south-of-the-border country of origin of the Brazilian.

breasticle: (n.) gender engineering gone horrifically wrong.

bribery: (n.) invisible grease that makes politics go round and round.

> *I never bought a man who wasn't for sale. —W.A. Clark*

Buddhism: (n.) doctrine that insists one can avoid suffering by *om*-ing long enough into one's asshole.

bullish: (adj.) term for describing a financial bully.

bureaucrat: (n.) career sadist who uses red tape to immobilize victims.

Bureau of Land Management (BLM): (n.) federal agency focused on saving rare aquatic snails while destroying hardworking people's lives and fomenting armed rebellion.

I believe there is someone out there watching us. Unfortunately, it's the government. —Woody Allen

byesexual: (n.) one who opts for abstinence.

Cabal buster: (n.) not necessarily feminist individual engaged in deconstructing the evil planetary control grid and restoring sovereignty and dignity to humanity.

It is hard for power to enjoy or incorporate humor and satire in its system of control. —Dario Fo

Calamityville Horror: (n.) reality show set in what is left of contemporary Detroit.

cancer: (n.) often deadly allergic reaction to modern life.

Candida. (n.) title of a witty medical treatise on yeast infections by Voltaire.

capitalism: (n.) economic theory based on the view that being poor should be punishable by death.

The road to success is paved with good Americans. —Yours Truly

capital punishment: (n.) BEING FORCED TO READ EMAIL CORRESPONDENCE IN ALL CAPS UNTIL ONE EXPIRES FROM THE EFFORT.

cargo cult: (n.) American public circa 2017 praying for products manufactured in China to be drone-dropped by Amazon.

cashless society: (n.) dystopian civilization where you can be sure the real terrorists have won.

Casual Tees: (n.) fitting name for a T-shirt store in time of war.

Catholicism: (n.) religion with more than a billion mind-controlled adherents willing to be absolved or condemned on the whim of a little wizened pontificator wearing a fishy hat.

census: (n.) being counted so we can be discounted.

What difference, at this point, does it make? —Hillary Clinton

channeling: (n.) making shit up without having to take personal responsibility.

It is useless to attempt to reason a man out of a thing he was never reasoned into. —Jonathan Swift

chaos theory: (n.) self-explanatory theoretical model postulating that out of chaos comes ... disorder.

character assassination: (n.) making an ass of oneself twice.

chemtrail: (n.) nothing to see up there day and night crisscrossing the sky and lingering for hours, folks, move along.

child sacrifice: (n.) crime of committing children to public education.

chorizo: (n.) spicy Spanish sausage over which many tears have been shed.

Christianity: (n.) force-fed faith based on a thorough lack of evidence that has proven to be more peaceful in concept than practice.

I like your Christ, I do not like your Christians. Your Christians are so unlike your Christ. —Mahatma Gandhi

Church of State: (n.) Big Government.

citation: (n.) ticket for misquoting someone en route.

civil disobedience: (n.) just saying hell no.

If a man does not keep pace with his companions, perhaps it is because he hears a different drummer. —Henry David Thoreau

civil rights: (n.) all those inalienable rights to remain civil rather than speak truth to power.

cocomutt: (n.) mixed-breed dog enjoying life on a tropical island.

codswallop: (n.) violent blow to the head with a saltwater fish.

coffee: (n.) caffeinated beverage God gave us to drink in the morning so we might resist the urge to crawl immediately back in bed.

college tuition: (n.) method of going into decades of debt to finance an outmoded education one can beat for free on the Internet.

> *We are students of words: we are shut up in schools, and colleges, and recitation-rooms, for ten or fifteen years, and come out at last with a bag of wind, a memory of words, and do not know a thing.*
> —*Ralph Waldo Emerson*

commercial: (n.) R-rated advertisement for drugs, sex or violence shown to minors on prime-time network television in America.

Common Core: (n.) teaching our kids that the wrong answers are right and the right ones are wrong.

> *Knowledge does not keep any better than fish.*
> —*Alfred North Whitehead*

commonism: (n.) social theory and practice for arriving at the lowest cultural decimator.

compartmentalization: (n.) solitary confinement of otherwise expansive minds in airtight, windowless boxes.

If the doors of perception were cleansed everything would appear to man as it is, infinite. For man has closed himself up till he sees all things through narrow chinks of his cavern. —William Blake

compound interest: (n.) banking industry enthusiasm to steal your money exponentially faster.

Congress: (n.) historically, a gathering of cons.

conjugal: (adj.) 1) etymologically, yoked together; 2) functionally, weighing each other down.

conscience: (n.) disqualifier for most intelligence work.

conservative: (adj.) term for describing an individual, group, party, idea, policy or law focused on eliminating considerations relative to conserving the common good.

Progress was all right. Only it went on too long. —James Thurber

conspiracy theorist: (n.) marginalized thinker with a better than average chance of being right on the money.

Constitution: (n.) all-important document adherence to which provides a measurement of the strength of America's immunity to internal parasites.

Stop throwing the Constitution in my face. It's just a goddamned piece of paper! —George W. Bush

Constitution-free Zone: (n.) United States of America under DHS occupation.

contempt of court: (n.) growing disdain of the two-tiered American justice system where the rich get an apology and the poor get a working vacation in the slammer.

convent: (n.) rant by which an inveterate fraudster gets something off his chest.

co-optation: (n.) stealth process by which farmers markets take over public spaces in the wee hours of the morning.

copulent: (adj.) term for describing a prurient police officer pigging out on doughnuts.

copyright: (n.) their right to clone you because they own you.

corporate personhood: (n.) legal hooey that leads to human depersonalization.

corporation: (n.) terrestrial equivalent of the Death Star.

corruption: (n.) type of rust that corrodes the heart of people who have lost their way.

Those who find ugly meanings in beautiful things are corrupt without being charming. This is a fault. Those who find beautiful meanings in beautiful things are the cultivated. For these there is hope.
—Oscar Wilde

Council on Foreign Relations (CFR): (n.) statist group of population control strategists for whom the idea of good relations with any people but their own is a foreign concept.

country music: (n.) moronic whining to make a fast buck.

crib: (n.) socialization tool for habituating infants to life imprisonment.

crime drama: (n.) fear-based behavior control in a police state that leads innocent viewers to worry—often subconsciously—that they themselves could be busted at any moment.

criminal justice: (n.) system in which the criminals mete out the justice.

crisis actor: (n.) anyone, such as a standing president, who plays a fake role in a staged terror incident.

critical thinking: (n.) always looking on the dark side.

critick: (n.) bloodsucker that feeds on artists' souls.

Don't pay any attention to what they write about you. Just measure it in inches. —Andy Warhol

crybully: (n.) evolved species of crybaby who, in lieu of brute force and physical intimidation, uses crocodile tears and political correctness to crush the opposition.

cryptocurrency: (n.) electronic money so mysterious no one can tell what it is or whence it comes.

cucumber: (n.) vegetable recommended by the US Department of Agriculture for live demos during Condom Ed in American elementary schools.

cunnilingus: (n.) clever speech used by politicians when hitting opponents below the belt.

cure for cancer: (n.) found, and suppressed by Big Pharma through coercion, bribery and assassination, every few years.

cynic: (n.) one who gets off the train before it reaches the station.

Scratch any cynic and you will find a disappointed idealist.
—George Carlin

dead white male: (n.) phrase meaning—in some fashionable intellectual circles—good white male.

death tax: (n.) just think about it for a minute.

debridement: (n.) painful erosion of a marriage typically culminating in divorce.

debt: (n.) financial fiction created by bankers, who have perfected the art of counterfeiting money, which they trade for real assets and sweat equity as they hoodwink free people into becoming slaves.

Give me control of a nation's money and I care not who makes its laws. —Mayer Amstel Rothschild

debt ceiling: (n.) national spending cap that has been removed so that now there is only clear blue sky crosshatched with drones and chemtrails.

Blessed are the young, for they will inherit the national debt. —Herbert Hoover

debt slave: (n.) just about everybody you know, unfortunately.

Deliberately Unconscious: (n.) psychologist Carl Jung's little-known phrase for describing somnambulists in these otherwise eye-opening times who seem to be making a focused effort to remain asleep.

His was a great sin who first invented consciousness. Let us lose it for a few hours. —F. Scott Fitzgerald

delusion: (v.) to extricate oneself from culturally ingrained illusions.

democracy: (n.) modern system of soft slavery presided over by demons.

*I believe we are on an irreversible trend toward more freedom and
democracy—but that could change. —Dan Quayle*

Democrat: (n.) Republican with half a heart.

denial: (n.) closed mind's safeguard against reality.

derivative: (n.) phony wealth concocted from funny money for the
bankers' sole benefit on their way to imploding the world economy.

devil: (n.) one who is saintly by hell's standards.

*The devil's finest trick is to persuade you that he does not exist.
—Charles Baudelaire*

diaper: (n.) makeshift flag of surrender when TSHTF.

dicktator: (n.) prick with absolute power.

disclosure: (n.) when they finally tell us everything and nothing
changes.

disenfranchisement: (n.) socially beneficial eradication of fast food chains.

disillusionment: (n.) when realizing that everything you thought was real is a mirage makes you physically ill.

It is not true that people stop pursuing dreams because they grow old, they grow old because they stop pursuing dreams.
—Gabriel García Márquez

disintermediation: (n.) removing the assholes from any system of exchange.

distopia: (n.) society gone wrong in which everyone relentlessly criticizes everybody else.

ditzyramb: (n.) sage expression of political pith.

diversity: (n.) politically correct insistence on fairness to unfair advantage.

divide and conquer: (n. or v.) planetary control strategy ad nauseam of the New World Order.

Hell is empty and all the devils are here. —William Shakespeare

dogma: (n.) hidebound manner of thinking that can lead to boundless bad karma.

dollar store: (n.) antiquated name for any store selling cheap items in the days when the dollar was actually worth something.

A nickel ain't worth a dime anymore. —Yogi Berra

doomsday: (n.) day of judgment that is somehow always tomorrow.

doublespeak: (n.) political stutter that typically occurs when the teleprompter malfunctions.

Dowist: (n.) blind believer in the stock market.

Don't gamble; take all your savings and buy some good stock and hold it till it goes up, then sell it. If it don't go up, don't buy it.
—Will Rogers

dream: (n.) nightly reprieve from unreality.

Dreams are real while they last, can we say more of life?
—Havelock Ellis

drone: (v.) what the US president does, on and on, with regard to establishing peace in our time while bombing the hell out of half the planet.

drone operator: (n.) see what happens to all such cogs in the war machine when freedom is back in fashion and the excuse "I was just following orders" no longer flies.

Monsters exist, but they are too few in number to be truly dangerous.
More dangerous are the common men, the functionaries ready to
believe and to act without asking questions. —Primo Levi

ebil: (n.) wickedness among Weebles.

economic forecast: (n.) ↓.

economic growth: (n.) viral infection in which the few get rich off the many while the planet withers.

economic reset: (n.) when the people get back all the wealth their elected and unelected officials pillaged from them.

Work is the curse of the drinking classes. —Oscar Wilde

ego: (n.) overblown sense of self-importance that, like the rectum, comes with being human.

Electric Universe: (n.) miniature desk display of our galaxy made—like our galaxy—in China.

emailsculation: (n.) insidious neutering of the modern male through computer technology.

empire collapse: (n.) pop some popcorn and settle in because you are living through it.

We live at the edge of the miraculous. —Henry Miller

end times: (n.) chaotic period filled with apocalyptic predictions just before things begin again.

The future is no more uncertain than the present. —Walt Whitman

enlightenment: (n.) rapid weight loss during a hunger strike leading to a life-changing epiphany.

entanglement: (n.) quantum physics term for when the sheets wrap around two bodies in space.

environmental pollution: (n.) China's largest export.

Environmental Protection Agency (EPA): (n.) federal agency tasked with safeguarding America's natural resources by dumping mining toxins into its rivers, one after another.

The good thing about forest fires is that, eventually, there's nothing left to burn. —Yours Truly

erectile dysfunction (ED): (n.) pandemic among modern males, who have difficulty identifying—much less standing up for—what they truly desire.

*I never trust a man unless I've got his pecker in my pocket.
—Lyndon B. Johnson*

European Union (EU): (n.) sneaky neologism for Fourth Reich.

evilution: (n.) process by which wickedness evolves and spreads.

We will, in fact, be greeted as liberators. —Dick Cheney

executive order: (n.) democracy's version of the monarch's decree—and just as erasable by revolution.

exile: (n.) one who does not feel at home on this planet.

expert: (n.) revered individual who knows a voluminous amount about virtually nothing.

The learned usually find themselves equipped to live in a world that no longer exists. —Eric Hoffer

exquizit: (n.) pimple of such delicate loveliness as to elicit profound enchantment.

extraterrestrial: (n.) surplus earthling.

Facebook: (n.) PR department of the NSA posing as a social media platform.

faction: (n.) any violent group that seeks to go to war over only a miniscule portion of the facts.

Give the people a new word and they think they have a new fact.
—Willa Cather

factotum: (n.) modern human encumbered by an extreme overload of facts.

Get your facts first, then you can distort them as you please.
—Mark Twain

faith: (n.) attitude often adopted when there is no hope.

false flag: (n.) American flag, sadly.

fanny-pack: (v.) to put on a few extra pounds during the holiday season.

farcicle: (n.) ridiculous popsicle.

far-right: (adj.) descriptive political term that, through time and usage, has had its middle word—*from*—replaced by a hyphen.

fartnight: (n.) two weeks of painful bloating.

fascism: (n.) government of the corporations, by the corporations, for the corporations.

Fascism is the stage reached after communism has proved an illusion.
—Friedrich Hayek

fast food: (n.) toxic crap from which smart people distance themselves as quickly as possible.

Fast food, designed to sap one's vitality bite by poisonous bite, is so called because it makes life pass fast. —Yours Truly

fatality: (n.) death by obesity.

fattist: (n.) similar to a sexist or racist—but much funnier.

fauxlio: (n.) urban myth that polio was eradicated by vaccination.

Don't be satisfied with stories, how things have gone with others. Unfold your own myth. —Rumi

fear porn: (n.) bad kind of porn.

Federal Emergency Management Agency (FEMA): (n.) disorganization organization purposed with making natural disasters much worse than they have to be.

Federal Reserve: (n.) if you think this institution is either federal or a reserve, perhaps you would be interested in some beachfront property on the Sea of Tranquility.

The curious task of economics is to demonstrate to men how little they really know about what they imagine they can design.
—*Friedrich Hayek*

fedora: (n.) Millennial Generation's contribution to the dustbin of fashion history already containing bullet bras, bell bottoms, tube socks, platform shoes, leg warmers, jean jackets, and flannel shirts.

feminism: (n.) raising up women by pushing down men.

fetish: (n.) anything, such as the stock market, falsely believed by primitive peoples to possess divine, magical or supernatural qualities.

Rationalism and doctrinairism are the disease of our time.
—*Carl Jung*

fiat currency: (n.) secondhand toilet paper used as a medium of exchange by people who have forgotten what money is.

It is no coincidence that the century of total war coincided with the century of central banking. —Ron Paul

Fibonacci sequence: (n.) set of rapidly escalating lies mathematically introduced by the mainstream media to pull the wool over your eyes.

firnication: (n.) how Christmas trees reproduce.

Flat Earth theory: (n.) controversial theory proponents of which maintain that life on this planet is unbearably tedious.

flip a bird: (v.) to use the middle finger to shoo an annoying pigeon or other bird away from one's food.

fluoride: (n.) artificial IQ suppressant, not to be confused with naturally occurring fluoride, produced as an industrial byproduct and added to public water supplies to, uh, oh, what was I saying?

fluoride face: (n.) out-to-lunch stare of the IQ-suppressed.

Food and Drug Administration (FDA): (n.) federal agency that keeps the food out and the drugs in.

food pyramid: (n.) invert for best results.

fool's gold: (n.) joker's good fortune.

Fools are my theme, let satire be my song. —Lord Byron

fracktious: (adj.) describes the behavior of shale oil industry shills toward anyone who highlights the obvious lunacy of poisoning the planet's groundwater.

fracking: (n.) sodomizing Mother Nature.

freedom of religion: (n.) right to foist one's religious beliefs on others.

free energy: (n.) coming soon to a cold fusion station near you.

freeloader: (n.) one who downloads a free ebook promising to review it but never does.

free speech: (n.) language often purchased at an exorbitant price.

None are more hopelessly enslaved than those who falsely believe they are free. —Johann Wolfgang von Goethe

frognostication: (n.) ability to foretell events in France.

funny bone: (n.) comical intercourse.

gag order: (n.) silencing truth for justice.

gallergy: (n.) hypersensitivity to fine art.

game theory: (n.) what if life really is a game and the solutions to all our problems, as well as the answer to all our desires, are written into the software?

Satire is a lesson, parody is a game. —*Vladimir Nabokov*

gaming: (n.) video method of teaching our children to kill indiscriminately and without conscience.

gangsta rap: (n.) acceptable contemporary hate speech where angels fear to tread and white lives don't matter.

genetically modified organism (GMO): (n.) member of the public who has regularly consumed the biotech industry's food products.

genetic engineering: (n.) when you get right down to it, how it all began.

geography: (n.) did you know many American high school students cannot point out America on a map? It appears some Kenyan students exhibit similar deficiencies.

I've now been in 57 states? I think one left to go. —*Barack Obama*

 **Germanate:** (v.) to grow little Germans.

germ theory: (n.) increasingly popular idea that there are germs in high places in many Western democracies that need to be wiped out by antibiotics for the health of the body politic to be restored.

gerrymandering: (n.) practice of relocating old people to different electoral districts to hijack elections.

glad-handing: (n.) heavy petting for personal or corporate gain.

global warming: (n.) result of excessive hot-air emissions by climate scientists.

glutton: (n.) one who knows it is better to overeat early than late.

God: (n.) fictitious biblical character like Jesus and Satan.

Go to Heaven for the climate, Hell for the company.
—Mark Twain

God-fearing: (adj.) phrase that should beg the question in the mind of any sentient being, "What kind of God are we talking about here?"

God particle: (n.) recently discovered subatomic particle theorized to be slightly larger and more elongated than the Goddess particle.

Not only is there no God, but try finding a plumber on Sunday.
—Woody Allen

Goldman Sucks: (n.) terminal rot at the financial core of the Big Apple.

good fortune: (n.) precarious state of grace when one manages to avoid ill fortune.

gossip: (n.) true when about another, false when about you.

Strong minds discuss ideas, average minds discuss events, weak minds discuss people. —Socrates

Greece: (n.) country where democracy was born—and died.

green thumb: (n.) hereditary mutation among members of banking families that makes for better grasping.

grope-on: (n.) coupon for attending a private party at the White House.

gullible: (adj.) susceptible to being hoodwinked by seafowl.

Reality is only a Rorschach ink-blot, you know. —Alan Watts

gun control: (n.) protecting the ~~aristocracy~~ government from its ~~serfs~~ citizens.

hate mail: (n.) universe's perverse way of urging you not to give up when you are doing something right.

hate speech: (n.) any speech those in power hate.

headphone: (n.) wireless communication microchip implanted in journalists' brains.

Turn on, tune in, drop out. —Timothy Leary

heart disease: (n.) fitting top killer in a civilization whose heart has hardened to the suffering of others.

hellocination: (n.) uncontrollable greeting of imaginary people.

herbivore: (n.) mammal that only consumes cannabis.

The biggest killer on the planet is stress and I still think the best medicine is and always has been cannabis. —Willie Nelson

heretick: (n.) one whose truth ticks off those in power.

It is dangerous to be right in matters on which the established authorities are wrong. —Voltaire

hermit: (n.) one who prefers his own company to no company at all.

heterophobia: (n.) currently acceptable variety of sexuality prejudice among the hip.

heterosexuality: (n.) passé.

high society: (n.) glitterati on coke.

himp: (v.) to hum while limping.

hindsight: (n.) viewing life from one's rear end.

hip pointer: (n.) fashionably trailblazing individual perambulating on crutches.

history: (n.) fiction disguised as fact written by shills bought and paid for by victorious pricks.

History is an account mostly false, of events mostly unimportant, which are brought about by rulers mostly knaves, and soldiers mostly fools. —*Ambrose Bierce*

Hollywood: (n.) where uplifting movie ideas go to die.

Holy Bible: (n.) monotheistic religious text so called because it is full of holes.

holy roller: (n.) devout gambler specializing in dice games.

Homeland Security: (n.) keeping the ~~Fatherland~~ Homeland safe ~~for~~ from the ~~shadow government~~ terrorists.

homeschool: (n.) domestic prophylactic against statist brainwashing.

There is no school equal to a decent home and no teacher equal to a virtuous parent. —Mahatma Gandhi

honor: (n.) human virtue absent among high-level bankers.

hopium: (n.) weaponized optimism.

horrorscope: (n.) when your astrology indicates it will be a really creepy day.

hospital: (n.) where the healthy go to get misdiagnosed and the sick go to get mistreated.

American's health care system is neither healthy, caring, nor a system. —Walter Cronkite

humanism: (n.) optimistic philosophy in the good old days before transhumanism when individuals still mattered and the world could still be saved.

husbandry: (n.) thrifty spousal management.

hyperinflation: (n.) pumping hot air into the economy until it explodes.

I: (pron.) new object of the preposition replacing "me" among American sportscasters.

Illwill: (n.) Goodwill's competition.

Itch-ing: (n.) ancient Chinese book detailing a system of divination for determining the location of skin rashes.

iffluenza: (n.) hypothetical illness.

ignorance: (n.) common sense in any society where right is wrong.

Scientific research is an implicit acknowledgement of ignorance.
—*Brendan D. Murphy*

illegal immigrant: (n.) until we live in a world without national borders, strictly correct term to describe an undocumented interloper.

imdogination: (n.) posing as one's furry friend.

imminent: (adj.) code word used by new age bloggers to signal that transformational events on a global scale have been—once again—unexpectedly and inexplicably delayed.

immunization: (n.) subcutaneous injection of neurotoxins and stealth pathogens designed to immunize the recipient from good health.

More people are now killed by vaccination than by smallpox.
—*George Bernard Shaw*

impeach: (v.) to give a basket of peaches to a standing president who has committed multiple felonies.

imperialism: (n.) process by which an empire's expansion is followed by contraction and, mercifully, implosion.

impolite conversation: (n.) sexy talk with the wrong person.

improper fraction: (n.) fraction that behaves badly.

indecision: (n.) there are times to do something and times to do nothing and now is one of those times.

When you come to a fork in the road, take it. —*Yogi Berra*

indentured servant: (n.) debt slave with false teeth.

Indigo Child: (n.) one who consumes too much colloidal silver early in life.

individual: (n.) human being who no longer matters.

The more the state "plans" the more difficult planning becomes for the individual. —*Friedrich Hayek*

indoctrination: (n.) transformation of an unaware participant in a study into a medical doctor.

Infernal Revenant Servant (IRS): (n.) unconstitutional private debt collection agency for the devil run by his American ambassador, the Federal Reserve, officially based in Puerto Rico and unofficially headquartered in the Vatican.

insinuation: (n.) annoying habit of religious fanatics who insist on inserting the topic of sin into polite conversation.

There is no sin except stupidity. —*Oscar Wilde*

insurance: (n.) mandatory "agreement" to pay a corporation that could care less about you a big chunk of your income no matter what.

insurrection: (n.) surgical removal of the oppressor's phallus.

intercourse: (n.) profound conversation between genitals.

Flirting is a promise of sexual intercourse without a guarantee.
—Milan Kundera

interplanetary: (adj.) pertaining to any of the highly advanced civilizations thriving inside the earth.

intestate: (adj.) word describing one who dies without testicles.

intestinal parasite: (n.) government regulator who bugs the crap out of you.

You can't make up anything anymore. The world itself is a satire.
All you're doing is recording it. —Art Buchwald

inventory: (n.) list of creative ideas.

Islamic State of Iraq and Syria (ISIS): (n.) us.

Israel: (n.) made-up country where real Jews are ruled by fake ones.

jabber: (n.) 1) religious talk; 2) vaccine giver.

job: (n.) paid alternative to pursuing one's calling.

> *Life is too short to waste being a productive member of society.*
> *—Yours Truly*

Jolly Roger: (n.) British slang for high-spirited copulation.

Jovial: (adj.) resembling a vengeful, philandering Greek god.

jubilee: (n.) jubilant shindig the world will have when the tyranny of debt finally dissolves.

juggernaut: (n.) astronaut with an unstoppable drinking problem.

"junk" DNA: (n.) according to mainstream scientists, nature's way of trashing us from the start.

Could there be an evolutionary purpose to "junk" DNA? Could it have hidden potential awaiting activation? Could it somehow activate the unused portion of our brain? —Yours Truly

jury nullification: (n.) helping indoctrinated judges get it right when there is no harm and thus no crime.

kamikaze: (n.) aerial suicide attack by the Bank of Japan against its own economy.

kangaroo court: (n.) sadly truthful description of virtually all American courts, starting with the Supreme Court of the United States.

The most dangerous man to any government is the man who is able to think things out ... Almost inevitably he comes to the conclusion that the government he lives under is dishonest, insane, intolerable.
—*H. L. Mencken*

karma: (n.) 1) lie dreamed up by those in power to trap the masses in a servile illusion; 2) Eastern equivalent of sin.

If you're a really mean person you're going to come back as a fly and eat poop. —Kurt Cobain

killer bee: (n.) bee madder than a hornet at humanity's wanton destruction of its natural habitat.

Kool-Aid: (n.) official beverage of the status quo.

The status quo sucks. —George Carlin

L

lack of authenticity: (n.) social disease that is quickly becoming an epidemic.

God has given you one face, and you make yourself another.
—William Shakespeare

laughing stock: (n.) unconventional beef broth made with funny bones.

All our best men are laughed at in this nightmare land.
—Jack Kerouac

Law of Attraction (LOA): (n.) new age distraction that celebrates self-centeredness as a spiritual virtue.

leap year: (n.) good time for taking calculated risks.

lexicon: (n.) 1) verbose fraudster; 2) politician.

liberal: (adj.) term for describing an individual, group, party, idea, policy or law focused on liberating the population from its ideals of personal freedom.

libertarian: (n.) opposite of a fascist.

Fascism wants Baptism coast to coast. —Ken Kesey

lie: (v.) what the president does when surreptitiously changing the placement of his golf ball.

I was not lying. I said things that later on seemed to be untrue.
—Richard Nixon

life: (n.) terminal condition that usually begins with vibrant health.

live off the land: (v.) to inhabit a floating city.

lobbyist: (n.) 1) sleazy middleman who traffics in bribes from corporations to politicians; 2) lucrative twilight career for former presidents and prime ministers.

lobotomy: (n.) job prerequisite for starting out as a journalist.

I'd rather have a bottle in front of me than a frontal lobotomy.
—Dorothy Parker

local media: (n.) endangered species in any former democracy, such as the United States, slipping into fascism.

Luddite: (n.) one who takes out frustration with the dehumanizing elements of modern life on uncomfortable shoes.

Lyme disease: (n.) chronic autoimmune condition that results from being bitten by an infected vaccine.

mad cow disease: (n.) bovine retribution for being exposed to antibiotics, growth hormones, pesticides and God knows what else by humans for far too long.

US beef is so tough because all the cows are mad. —*Yours Truly*

Manifest Density: (n.) doctrine requiring that American expansionism must be accompanied by diminution of the American intellect.

You teach a child to read, and he or her will be able to pass a literacy test. —George W. Bush

marijuana: (n.) hallucinatory substance with wide-ranging medicinal properties that was made illegal because it makes everything better—*and we can't have that.*

When I was in England, I experimented with marijuana a time or two, and I didn't like it. I didn't inhale it, and never tried it again.
—Bill Clinton

market rigging: (n.) financial chains, ropes and other torture devices used to punish the slaves on the ship of fools that is the global economy.

 Martian law: (n.) current legal system.

Marxism: (n.) deliberate destruction of difference resulting in the death of humor and demise of culture.

If anything is certain, it is that I myself am not a Marxist.
—Karl Marx

masculine napkin: (n.) hygienic cloth used by a man to wipe his brow during periods of elevated stress in a world that has been cleverly filched from him.

masculinity: (n.) lost art of having balls.

mass arrests: (n.) with any luck, they will soon start at the very top.

mass hypnosis: (n.) public education.

mass hysteria: (n.) collective insanity that is easy enough to whip up when you control the media.

mass shooting: (n.) forced vaccination.

mass surveillance: (n.) looking out for everyone's neighbor.

"mass" whatever: (n.) typically, something designed to traumatize or limit the people.

materialist: (n.) one whose dogmatic opinions, when the multidimensional truth of reality is finally laid bare, will be revealed as immaterial.

Belief in a mechanistic universe is a modern superstition.
—Walter Heitler

maturity: (n.) recognition of one's own jaw-dropping stupidity very late in the game.

mediumship: (n.) ship that is neither large nor small.

mental hospital: (n.) place of incarceration run by the crazies.

The test of a first-rate intelligence is the ability to hold two opposed ideas in mind at the same time, and still retain the ability to function. —F. Scott Fitzgerald

mercury: (n.) neurotoxic "silver" material for filling cavities preferred by genocidal dentists everywhere.

merkin: (n.) US citizen born and raised in the Deep South.

metoob: (n.) 1) YouTube knockoff; 2) narcissistic boob.

microaggression: (n.) tiny, often unintentional insult blown completely out of proportion and socially weaponized by a crybully.

microeconomics: (n.) when the amount of capital you have to work with can only be seen with a microscope.

Why, look at me. I've worked my way up from nothing to a state of extreme poverty. —*Groucho Marx*

Millennial: (n.) one who is out of work and lives in her parents' basement but still votes Democrat.

miracle: (n.) now would be a good time for a really big one.

misdirection: (n.) botched opportunity to score.

miseducation: (n.) nostalgia for a classical liberal arts foundation.

The paradox of education is precisely this; that as one begins to become conscious one begins to examine the society in which he is being educated. —*James Baldwin*

misgovernment: (n.) any form of government.

History, in general, only informs us what bad government is. —*Thomas Jefferson*

money laundering: (n.) time-honored banking technique for removing bloodstains from the currency.

monoglot: (n.) 1) one who barely manages to speak his own language; 2) average American.

Your average American is below average. —Yours Truly

Monsanto: (n.) second most hated corporation on the planet behind only the one that poses as the USA.

moral rectitude: (n.) annoying habit of having a straight stick stuck up your ass.

Do the right thing. It will gratify some people and astonish the rest.
—Mark Twain

mortgage: (n.) borrower's contract with *Harry Potter*'s Voldemort used to "purchase" a house one will never own.

motherfracker: (n.) exactly what everyone in the shale oil industry is.

musepaper: (n.) proposed term for inspirational news genre to which the fearmongering media should aspire to avoid obsolescence.

Once you embark on a road of imagination and creating, all bets are off. All preconceptions about what you must do, make, think, assume, and believe are yesterday's news. —Jon Rappoport

Muslim: (n.) most easily outraged of all religious fanatics—which is saying a lot.

mystery school: (n.) esoteric academy where nobody knows what the hell they are teaching.

mystickle: (n.) enjoyable irritation one feels when spirituality is funny.

mythology: (n.) synonym for history employed by the victors in a cultural struggle to marginalize the true story of the vanquished.

naanite: (n.) microscopic piece of Indian bread typically made with garlic.

nailbiter: (n.) suicided mid-level banker who knew too much about the child trafficking and RICO crimes his bosses masterminded.

narcotrafficking: (n.) elephant in the room in most discussions of what keeps the New World Order able to finance all its evildoings.

National Aeronautics and Space Administration (NASA): (n.) front for the real space program headquartered inside Uranus.

National Collegiate Athletic Association (NCAA): (n.) organization devoted to upholding the amateur purity of collegiate athletics by allowing unpaid student athletes to be turned into cash cows for corporations and universities.

National Rifle Association (NRA): (n.) organization dedicated to defending Americans from their government.

If the American people ever find out what we have done, they will chase us down the streets and lynch us. —George H.W. Bush

National Football League (NFL): (n.) PR firm for the military-industrial complex—when not Running from the Cure.

National Public Radio (NPR): (n.) propaganda that gives you a warm and fuzzy feeling while you surrender your inalienable rights.

nation state: (n.) arbitrary geographical area drawn on a map by God knows who with laws designed to keep its citizens inside the lines.

naturist: (n.) nude hiker typically from Germany or Scandinavia, where they like things like nude hiking.

naturopathy: (n.) heretical belief, nevertheless substantiated by centuries of observation, that the body is often capable of healing itself when spared the leechcraft of fashionable medicine.

The art of medicine consists in amusing the patient while nature cures the disease. —Voltaire

naval-gazer: (n.) one who becomes lost in contemplation of ships' reflections.

 **naybor:** (n.) contrarian guy next door.

necroromancer: (n.) novelist who takes advantage of the unawakened's thirst for gratuitous violence to make a killing.

neocon: (n.) 1) member of an organized crime syndicate masquerading as a political party using Jesus as a front man; 2) Hitler Youth.

There is nothing more frightful than ignorance in action. —Johann Wolfgang von Goethe

new age: (n.) life stage that precedes old age.

Old age is the most unexpected of all things that can happen to a man. —James Thurber

niggle: (v.) to giggle uncontrollably in the nude.

no: (interj.) word We the People need to relearn before we all become yes-men.

Just say no. —Nancy Reagan

noise pollution: (n.) evening news.

non-governmental organization (NGO): (n.) ostensibly independent agency controlled by the NWO used to infiltrate target countries in order to foster social unrest, destruction of democracy, and—if all goes according to plan—installation of a vassal state.

nosey: (adj.) oversensitive to the smell of bullshit.

nudetrition: (n.) nourishment enjoyed in the buff.

Nuremberg Trials: (n.) precursor to an even more explosive exposé of Nazis in high places among us that could happen any day now in the good old USofA.

These are the times that try men's souls. —Thomas Paine

oligarpy: (n.) world government according to money.

oming pigeon: (n.) meditative bird.

oops: (n.) term for those rare but wonderful occasions when a politician utters what she is really thinking.

> *We have to pass the [health care] bill so that you can find out what's in it. —Nancy Pelosi*

open-source: (adj.) phrase describing a technology for giving it away electronically to the people while sticking it to the Man.

opine: (v.) to whimper on opium.

O-pression: (n.) being weighed down from watching too much *Oprah*.

Osama bin Laden: (n.) former CIA operative currently partying with Elvis and Jim Morrison in Borneo.

out of work: (adj.) phrase indicating there are no more jobs left.

It's a recession when your neighbor loses his job; it's a depression when you lose yours. —Harry Truman

outsourcing: (n.) other than dropping a nuclear bomb, most straightforward way of destroying an economy.

You work three jobs? Uniquely American, isn't it? I mean, that is fantastic that you're doing that. —George W. Bush

oxymoron: (n.) one who wastes so much breath saying idiotic things he runs out of oxygen.

pacifist: (n.) one who lives near the Pacific hoping to be protected by someone else.

paid disinformant: (n.) mainstream journalist.

paint bomb: (n.) artist's tool replacing the brush in much modern art.

paparazzi: (n.) antipasti made with fallen idols.

parannoyed: (adj.) state of mind of many so-called conspiracy theorists, who know more is going on behind the scenes than is acknowledged and are fed up with those in denial.

I am incapable of conceiving infinity, and yet I do not accept finity.
—Simone de Beauvoir

passport: (n.) official form of internationally accepted ID required by law to be left at any scene where one has committed an act of terrorism.

pasteurization: (n.) historically recent technique for taking food that nature intended to be consumed alive and killing it.

patriarchy: (n.) when bad men do evil things to good people.

Patriot Act: (n.) fascist legislation of the true terrorists, by the true terrorists, for the true terrorists.

 **patriotism:** (n.) crime of loving one's country.

A thing is not necessarily true because a man dies for it.
—Oscar Wilde

peace of mind: (n.) inner calm that comes from speaking one's mind.

pedophilia: (n.) Satanic lust by many in power for tiny young feet.

He was either a pediatrician or a pedophile, I can't remember which.
—Yours Truly

peer review: (n.) institutional gatekeeper strategy designed to screen out inconvenient truths from mainstream acceptance.

peer-to-peer: (n.) electronic transmission of social diseases.

penicity: (n.) propensity to be a real dick.

perfume: (n.) petroleum-based poison used mainly by women to surround themselves with a pleasant-smelling cloud of toxicity.

Happiness is a perfume you cannot pour on others without getting
some on yourself. —Ralph Waldo Emerson

pestimism: (n.) habit of making a nuisance of oneself by always seeing the glass as half empty.

Petrodollar System: (n.) decades-old scam—thankfully coming to an end—in which nations have been forced to purchase oil with blood money.

pillow talk: (n.) last resort when no one else understands you.

pink: (n.) color used of late on cancer awareness attire that appears to be just another shade of $green$.

pissport: (n.) British slang for license to go drinking.

Planet X: (n.) newly discovered sex tourism destination where everything is X-rated.

please state: (n.) any formerly repressive state in which the government's mercenaries have descended from their armored vehicles, laid down their automatic weapons, and engaged the public in polite dialogue.

Pledge of Allegiance: (n.) Nazi-style potty training behind the servile American mind.

Either America will destroy ignorance or ignorance will destroy the United States. —W.E.B. Du Bois

Plunge Protection Team: (n.) financial plumbing group showing cracks while trying to plug up the holes.

plutocrat: (n.) someone living in a high-security compound at the edge of the solar system who makes up the rules for the rest of us.

If somebody else is making the rules for you, no matter how good the payoff is for you, you're being conned. —Jon Rappoport

political correction: (n.) long-overdue incarceration and reeducation of our so-called leaders.

political correctness (PC): (n.) latest fad in mind control.

Where all think alike, no one thinks very much. —Walter Lippmann

political reform: (n.) saying something to avoid doing something.

political theater: (n.) precisely what politics is.

People say satire is dead. It's not dead; it's alive and living in the White House. —Robin Williams

ponerography: (n.) graphic depiction in words or images of the genocide of defenseless peoples by psychopaths posing as world leaders.

Ponzi scheme: (n.) Western financial system.

pooped: (adj.) exhausted from a bout of the scoots.

pop culture: (n.) so called because it is empty and susceptible to implosion like a balloon.

pop music: (n.) sonic vomit genetically modified to sound like candy.

populist: (n.) any leader who is unpopular with the Global Elite.

pork chop: (n.) sucker punch by a dirty cop.

POVerty: (n.) unfortunately myopic perspective of one who is born poor.

pragmatist: (n.) anyone with a shrunken sense of possibility.

pragnant: (adj.) knocked up with a utilitarian idea.

Propositions arrived at by pure logical means are completely empty as regards reality. —Albert Einstein

predictive programming: (n.) when they tell us they are going to shaft us before they screw us.

preemptive strike: (n.) killing them first so you can die minutes later.

premeditation: (n.) warm-up meditation.

preoccupation: (n.) job one does before going to work.

prepper: (n.) one who logically prepares when faced with reality despite the incessant propaganda that such preparations are illogical.

presstitution: (n.) high-profile career spent performing tricks in public as a mainstream journalist.

prevert: (n.) one who begins life already corrupted.

Sick and perverted always appeals to me. —Madonna

price discovery: (n.) knowledge that causes severe sticker shock in a hyperinflating economy.

primitivism: (n.) belief that other people are less advanced.

primogeniture: (n.) patriarchal law stating that the one who dies with the most indentured servants triumphs.

prison-industrial-military-pharmaceutical complex (PIMP): (n.) America circa 2017.

prison reform: (n.) what will happen when our nonviolent "offenders" are released to make room for those who should be incarcerated: our violent "leaders."

privilege: (n.) anything granted that should be a right.

progressive: (n.) authoritarian in sheeple's clothing.

prohibition: (n.) criminalizing whatever makes people happy.

Prohibition is the trigger of crime. —Ian Flemming

Project Blue Ball: (n.) diabolical plot to holographically project sex-starved aliens against the backdrop of chemtrails in our skies to frighten people into accepting a single planetary baseball team.

propserity: (n.) illusory appearance of wealth.

prosaic: (adj.) term for characterizing life on Prozac.

prostrate cancer: (n.) soul-destroying condition most prevalent in those who blindly submit to authority.

pseudo science: (n.) official science.

Popular medicine and popular morality belong together and ought not to be evaluated so differently as they still are: both are the most dangerous pseudo-sciences. —Friedrich Nietzsche

psi: (v.) what those with personal experience of the paranormal do when skeptics with no such experience but extremely rigid opinions go into knee-jerk debunking.

psychiatriste: (n.) someone who, sadly, needs to have her head examined.

The only difference between the sane and the insane is that the sane have the power to lock up the insane. —Hunter S. Thompson

Psyops: (n.) modern creature of mass distraction related to the Cyclops but with many more eyes.

We'll know our disinformation program is complete when everything the American public believes is false. —William Casey

psychobabble: (n.) contemporary intellectual discourse which makes the mouth move in mesmerizing circles.

psychopath: (n.) inhumane route taken by nearly everyone in a position of power.

puberty: (n.) tender age at which UK citizens become alcoholics.

Public Enema Numero Uno: (n.) whoever happens to be in charge in Mexico.

This town needs an enema! —Jack Nicholson as the Joker

pundit: (n.) political propagandist who communicates primarily in puns.

puppet: (n.) politician doubled over grasping his ankles while suspended high above reality from shadowy strings armored with blackmail.

putter: (n.) US president.

putting zoo: (n.) cage full of furry golfers.

quack: (n.) duck posing as a medical doctor.

The reason some ducks peter out is that they mate for life.
—Yours Truly

quagmire: (n.) bipartisan political system from which a nauseating stench arises.

quantitative easing (QE): (n.) financial equivalent of slapping a band-aid on a brain tumor.

It is well enough that people of the nation do not understand our banking and monetary system, for if they did, I believe there would be a revolution before tomorrow morning. —Henry Ford

quark: (n.) subatomic fart.

queef: (n.) tropical fruit related to the quince.

quick fix: (n.) rushed rigging by bankers of crumbling financial markets.

quim: (n.) whimsical thought of sex.

Virtue is persecuted by the wicked more than it is loved by the good. —Miguel de Cervantes

quixotic: (n.) easy lay from a faraway land.

R

race-baiting: (n.) recently perfected form of political phishing.

race card: (n.) trump played when discrimination or reverse discrimination flushes the jokers out into the open.

racketeering: (n.) surprisingly common substitute for tennis among high-level bankers.

radical Islam: (n.) do you really need a prophet to tell you this is the antithesis of a religion of peace?

random number generator: (n.) malfunctioning nonrandom number generator.

rant: (n.) tiny bitch with more bark than bite.

My recipe for dealing with anger and frustration: set the kitchen timer for twenty minutes, cry, rant, and rave, and at the sound of the bell, simmer down and go about business as usual. —Phyllis Diller

rationalism: (n.) scientific philosophy in which truth is carefully rationed.

The wallpaper with which the men of science have covered the world of reality is falling to tatters. —Henry Miller

rebuttal: (n.) rapid doubling of the size of one's derriere from sitting on it in a cubicle day after day.

refugee: (n.) anyone seeking asylum from the FEMA camp known as planet Earth.

regime change: (n.) change for the better to be anticipated enthusiastically in many Western instances.

religion: (n.) 1) time-honored method of brainwashing; 2) aborted spirituality.

Frisbeetarianism is the belief that when you die, your soul goes up on the roof and gets stuck. —George Carlin

reincarnation: (n.) giving the gift of cheap flowers a second time.

Republican: (n.) Democrat with half a pair of balls.

reverse discrimination: (n.) bigotry for the nondiscriminatory.

revolution: (n.) making a circle from the old despot to the new one.

*Listen, the next revolution is gonna be a revolution of ideas.
—Bill Hicks*

ribbing: (n.) joking around with a condom.

Russia: (n.) in a bizarre reversal since the days of the Soviet Union, leader of the free world.

sacred femininity: (n.) true expression of female essence of which today's "scarred" femininity is but a distorted echo.

sacred masculinity: (n.) in the modern era should be spelled "scared" masculinity.

sacrifice for one's country: (n.) only worth it if the country is worth it.

I wouldn't be caught dead sacrificing myself for this country.
—Yours Truly

"safe space": (n.) First Amendment-eviscerating figment of today's utopian collegiate imagination where, in a dystopian twist, free speech is anything but safe.

salvationism: (n.) long con.

sardonic: (n.) sarcastic thought used to forget an unpleasant memory.

Sassquatch: (n.) extremely tall crypto-hominid with a potty mouth.

Satanism: (n.) official state religion of the City of London, Vatican City, and Washington, DC.

It would be absurd if we did not understand both angels and devils, since we invented them. —John Steinbeck

Saudi Arabia: (n.) medieval kingdom where the royalty enjoys subjugating women and browbeating the populace bedecked in headgear fashioned from tablecloths purloined from the corner deli.

schizofrenetic: (adj.) hearing voices at a frantic pace.

Why is it that when we talk to God we're said to be praying, but when God talks to us we're schizophrenic? —*Lily Tomlin*

scientist: (n.) priest of the Church of Scienceology.

sci-finance: (n.) make-believe monetary system that artificially enslaves the planet through extraterrestrial technology.

Séance: (n.) Beyoncé's even more occult half-sister.

Second Amendment to the US Constitution (revised): (n.) A well-regulated minutia, being necessary to the security of a police state, the right of the people to weep with bare arms, shall not be unhinged.

It's July 4th here in the United States, and a lot of people are off today. Way off. —*Yours Truly*

seer: (v.) to burn oneself or another through a vision.

The small part of ignorance that we arrange and classify we give the name of knowledge. —*Ambrose Bierce*

self-esteem: (n.) quality found in great abundance in those who esteem themselves too highly.

self-massage: (n.) masturbation for health.

sense of humor: (n.) arguably the most important quality of a free society.

serfdumb: (n.) neofeudal citizenship in a New World Order where the slaves are too stupid to perceive their chains.

If you are silent about your pain, they'll kill you and say you enjoyed it. —Zora Neale Hurston

sexual inequality: (n.) implicit rule that one of the sexes must always be on top.

shadow government: (n.) real government by really evil people behind the dog and pony show for baby boomers and morons that plays on CNN.

shadow side: (n.) self you encounter when you do not look in the mirror.

Knowing your own darkness is the best method for dealing with the darknesses of other people. —Carl Jung

sheeple: (n.) condescending term for the herdable masses that, unfortunately, has more than a little ring of truth.

If you expect nothing from anybody, you're never disappointed. —Sylvia Plath

shill: (n.) coiffed anchorman with a shit-eating grin.

shortcoming: (n.) disappointment felt when one comes too early and not very far.

Shower Channel: (n.) better, and wetter, than the Weather Channel.

siren song: (n.) sound of milk frothing for one's morning latté.

skeptic: (n.) one who thinks with a limp and speaks without thinking.

It is evident that skepticism, while it makes no actual change in man, always makes him feel better. —Ambrose Bierce

skeptic tank: (n.) final resting place of the Newtonian worldview.

Beware the man with one book. —*Arab Proverb*

skin tag: (n.) injectable tracking microchip for human animals.

smart meter: (n.) cancer-causing surveillance Trojan Horse that shows just how dumb people are to allow one anywhere near their home.

smartphone: (n.) technological workaround for thinking.

smurfing: (n.) micropayment strategy used by bankers to bypass having to report that their willies are growing shorter annually.

snark: (n.) drug cop with a bad attitude.

Sneaker of the House: (n.) contrary to current usage, this is the correct spelling.

social contract: (n.) allegedly binding agreement with so-called authorities no one can recall having signed.

socialism: (n.) when all members of society are required by law to be social at all times.

I don't know half of you half as well as I should like; and I like less than half of you half as well as you deserve. —J.R.R. Tolkien

social justice in America: (n.) when good things happen to bad people and bad things happen to good people.

social media: (n.) any of various online networking platforms for users with no real friends.

sovereignty: (n.) until we individually have it, we collectively have nothing.

War is peace. Freedom is slavery. Ignorance is strength.
—George Orwell

speak one's mind: (v.) to offend somebody.

spliffy: (adj.) fashionably stoned.

When you smoke herb, it reveals you to yourself. —Bob Marley

spoiler: (n.) bad apple who ruins everything for everybody until there are no spoils left to go around.

Standard American Diet: (n.) really, truly and literally SAD.

starseed: (n.) any seed that has fallen extremely far from the tree.

straight: (adj.) possibly but not necessarily narrow.

stress: (n.) nature's tax on the modern lifestyle.

Ironically enough, the only people who can hold up indefinitely under the stress of modern war are psychotics. Individual insanity is immune to the consequences of collective insanity. —Aldous Huxley

student loan: (n.) uneducated move that mortgages one's best years for a BS degree in an economy where there are no jobs.

suffrage: (n.) right to suffer the consequences (often the same) of voting for either party in a general election.

If voting changed anything, they'd make it illegal.
—Emma Goldman

Super Bowl Halftime Show: (n.) open house at the Church of Satan.

superiority: (n.) attitude that inevitably reveals one's inferiority.

suppresso: (n.) beverage of questionable derivation served at Starbucks in a dictatorship.

sweatshop: (v.) to get a workout while window-shopping.

swinger: (n.) long-armed tropical monkey with a roving eye.

talking head: (n.) lascivious speech punctuating oral sex.

Tantricise: (n.) like Jazzercise, but better.

tantrum sex: (n.) excellent way to raise *kundalini* when pissed off.

taste: (n.) ability to tell the difference between enough and more than enough.

tax aversion: (n.) instinctual dislike of being mugged by one's government at pen point.

We are going to take things away from you on behalf of the common good. —Hillary Clinton

technology: (n.) potentially crippling material crutch opted for in lieu of what humans probably can learn to do through their own consciousness.

teleprompter: (n.) ubiquitous device used for telepathic mind control of newscasters and presidents.

Tenth Amendment to the US Constitution (ratified in 1791 and ignored ever since): (n.) The powers not delegated to the United States by the Constitution, nor prohibited by it to the States, are reserved to the States respectively, or to the people.

terrorism: (n.) desperate act of revenge after your enemy has destroyed everything and everybody you love.

terrorist: (n.) law-abiding citizen.

Our enemies are innovative and resourceful, and so are we. They never stop thinking about new ways to harm our country and our people, and neither do we. —*George W. Bush*

testosterone: (n.) fuel for monster trucks.

texting: (n.) obsessive-compulsive habit performed while driving in rush hour traffic for most explosive results.

theater of the absurd: (n.) avant-garde politics.

third eye: (n.) vestigial ESP gland that lies dormant in most people located between the second and fourth eyes.

Watching television is like taking black spray paint to your third eye. —*Bill Hicks*

Tikul Pikul: (n.) ancient Mayan site dedicated to fertility rites.

tipping point: (n.) phrase coined in landmark scientific study showing that when one tenth of a herd of cows mentally accepts being knocked to the ground, the entire herd magically tips over.

titillate: (v.) to celebrate with one's breast friends.

I've never had the honor of being a best man, but I've always had the pleasure of being a breast man. —Yours Truly

tolerance: (n.) allowing other people to do what you want them to.

traditional family values: (n.) doublespeak made infamous by George H.W. Bush that celebrates subservience, consumerism, dogmatic faith, patriarchy, ethnocentrism, blind obedience to authority, and that sort of thing.

 **tranny:** (n.) recent slang for First Lady.

You know Michelle is a tranny? —Joan Rivers

Transcendentalism: (n.) highbrow philosophical strategy for overcoming the world's bullshit.

transgendered: (adj.) wishy-washy not so much in one's private life but as concerns the life of one's privates.

transhumanism: (n.) turning people who have not already been transformed into robots into machines.

transparency: (n.) when those on the inside can see clearly what those on the outside cannot.

This is the most transparent administration in history.
—Barack Obama

Transportation Security Administration (TSA): (n.) officially authorized groping by the nation of you and your relations.

transubstantiation: (n.) use of one lie to support another.

trauma response: (n.) shock followed by a wave of numbness that occurs as a result of unexpected exposure to network news.

travesty: (n.) mobile caricature.

treason: (n.) crime against one's country and its people punishable by reelection.

The high office of the president has been used to foment a plot to destroy America's freedom, and before I leave office I must inform the citizens of this plight. —John F. Kennedy

tree hugger: (n.) one who, understandably, prefers trees to most people.

I only go out to get me a fresh appetite for being alone. —Lord Byron

tribulation: (n.) scary moment when the whole tribe shakes.

trigger: (v.) to cause the shadow side to erupt in an ostensibly sane person or group.

triptofan: (n.) turkey who prefers drugs over reality.

troll: (n.) anyone, paid or otherwise, who writes a disparaging online review of this dictionary.

Trumpette: (n.) Atlantic City call girl with a ridiculous wig.

truth: (n.) opposite of a lie—except in the increasingly normal instances when a lie is considered the truth.

Truth is treason in the empire of lies. —*Ron Paul*

truther: (n.) one who is just asking too darn much.

The truth may be stretched thin, but it never breaks, and it always surfaces above lies, as oil floats on water. —*Miguel de Cervantes*

turd eye: (n.) body part skeptics with a speech impediment use to shit all over those who can actually see the magic and mystery of the multiverse.

turn signal: (n.) optional in Southern states.

turning the other cheek: (n.) backside screen in basketball.

twerk: (n.) tweet with perks.

Twitter: (n.) social network for the illiterate.

two-party system: (n.) methodology of screwing us from the top and bottom simultaneously.

There can be no liberty for a community which lacks the means by which to detect lies. —Walter Lippmann

Tyrantosaurus rex: (n.) Queen Elizabeth, who really is a ~~reptilian~~ dinosaur.

𝔘

Unaffordable Unfair Act: (n.) proposed new name for the Affordable Care Act.

Un-American: (n.) any of a growing number of individuals who have voluntarily renounced US citizenship.

unbridled: (adj.) happily divorced.

unidentified floating orgasm (UFO): (n.) sex with a stranger in a hot air balloon.

United States Patent and Trademark Office (USPTO): (n.) burial place of genuinely revolutionary inventions the Powers That Be cannot otherwise control.

unity consciousness: (n.) belief that there is only one mind that matters: one's own.

un-ity consciousness: (n.) destructive mindset that seeks to screw up everything in sight.

> *Students achieving Oneness will move on to Twoness.*
> *—Woody Allen*

unlightenment: (n.) hiding your brilliance under a bushel.

> *Enlightenment typically begins with a pinch of anger and a sprinkle of rage. —Yours Truly*

US domestic policy: (n.) imprison all the dark people.

Useless: (n.) overrated modernist novel by James Joyce about a bloke wandering around Dublin with too much time on his hands.

useless eater: (n.) sports star filming a fast food commercial.

US foreign policy: (n.) kill all the dark people.

usury: (n.) liking to use and/or be used by others.

Neither a borrower nor a lender be. —William Shakespeare

vagrant: (n.) one who speaks in ambiguous circles.

vegabond: (n.) hitchhiker bound for Las Vegas.

vegan: (n.) individual from the Vega star system with an innate desire to consume people who eat meat.

veganism: (n.) new age religion in which meat replaces the devil.

Vegas nerve: (n.) poker face.

vegetable: (n.) one who has watched or participated in too many presidential debates.

I thought how unpleasant it is to be locked out—and I thought how it is worse, perhaps, to be locked in. —Virginia Woolf

vegetarian: (n.) one who consumes only vegetables including eggs, fish, and sometimes chicken.

Superficial people are like planets, always orbiting. —Yours Truly

vergin: (n.) one who is constantly on the verge of the first time.

Viagra: (n.) so a geezer can perform like Niagara.

victimless crime: (n.) chew on that for a second.

𝔄

waffle: (n.) breakfast of politicians.

Opinions are made to be changed—or how is truth to be got at?
—Lord Byron

wager: (n.) bet placed on the warmongers among us.

wait gain: (n.) what happens when welfare lines grow longer.

wake-believe: (n.) pretense of being awake.

Wall Street: (n.) if we are going to build a wall to protect ourselves from our enemies, let us use logic and start here.

wanton: (n.) lewd Chinese noodle stuffed with factory-raised pork.

war chest: (n.) Kim Kardashian in plate armor.

War on Drugs: (n.) battle waged against often harmless substances by people who are clearly on drugs.

I was under medication when I made the decision to burn the tapes.
—Richard Nixon

War on Terror: (n.) battle waged against mostly harmless people by people who are clearly on drugs.

The mind of America is seized by a fatal dry rot.
—Hunter S. Thompson

weapon of mass destruction (WMD): (n.) public faith in elected officials hell-bent on waging war for entirely made-up reasons.

Those who can make you believe absurdities can make you commit atrocities. —Voltaire

Whirled Health Organization (WHO): (n.) international agency that uses toxic vaccination campaigns to put the health of entire nations in a blender.

whistleblower: (n.) truth-telling patriot who exposes the lying sons of bitches in our midst.

Being called a traitor by Dick Cheney is the highest honor you can give an American. —Edward Snowden

whitewash: (n. or v.) *shhh*, microaggressive term.

 **widget:** (n.) diminutive email-order bride.

wisened: (adj.) shriveled by the wisdom of experience.

World Economic Forum: (n.) annual convention in Davos, Switzerland, where the Global Elite congratulate each other on being sickeningly wealthy as a result of having deliberately engineered a diseased planet.

The rich are different from you and me. —F. Scott Fitzgerald

wormhole: (n.) hole made in the ground by a worm that allows it to travel instantaneously from one side of the earth to the other— which explains why worms exist practically everywhere.

wrestitution: (n.) forcefully taking back what has been stolen.

xanado: (n.) cheesy hairstyle.

Xanax: (n.) prescription anti-anxiety medication that makes one immune to satire.

I'm sure I'd feel a lot worse if I weren't under such heavy sedation.
—David St. Hubbins

X-Men **movies:** (n.) transhumanist propaganda for the New World Order.

X-ray: (n.) radiation beam used by the good men and women of the TSA to peer beneath passengers' underwear.

xylophone: (n.) musical instrument for the nonmusical.

The world was simply and sheerly divided into "the aware," those who had the experience of being vessels of the divine, and a great mass of "the unaware," "the unmusical," "the unattuned."
—Tom Wolfe

X-rated: (adj.) nowadays, PG.

yapper: (n.) small, furry news correspondent.

Yes We Can: (interj.) Newspeak for *No You Can't.*

A lie can travel half way around the world while the truth is putting on its shoes. —Mark Twain

youphony: (n.) complacency with respect to the sound of one's own superficiality.

youtopia: (n.) perfect society with hi-tech communication tools where everything is about you.

Find joy and solace in the simple, and cultivate your utopia by feeling the Tao in every cubic inch of space. —Wayne Dyer

zapper: (n.) handheld electronic device for identifying and eliminating human parasites.

Zeitgeist: (n.) any era's predominant dogma before it is replaced by the next era's predominant dogma.

Zelig: (n.) classic Woody Allen mockumentary foretelling the lives and times of Barack Obama.

A zebra does not change its spots. —Al Gore

zero: (n.) approximate value of the US dollar in the not-so-distant future.

Zika virus: (n.) latest CDC-sponsored fearmongering buzzword out of the same half-baked cookbook for concocting mass vaccination and martial law as the SARS, ebola, West Nile virus, swine flu, bird flu and MERS hoaxes.

zombie apocalypse: (n.) Wal-Mart on Black Friday.

ZZ Top: (n.) godfathers of the modern Beard Movement.

It ain't over till it's over. —Yogi Berra

ABOUT YOURS TRULY

Sol Luckman is a pioneering ink painter whose work has been featured on mainstream book covers, the fast-paced trading game *Bazaar*, and at least one female leg last spotted in Australia. He is also a bestselling nonfiction author whose books on health and wellness include *Conscious Healing* and *Potentiate Your DNA*. His visionary novel, *Snooze: A Story of Awakening*, winner of the 2015 National Indie Excellence Award for New Age Fiction, is the coming-of-age tale of one extraordinary boy's awakening to the world-changing reality of his dreams. Read Sol's blog and sign up to receive his Devilishly Clever Word of the Day free in your inbox at **www.CrowRising.com**.

Could it be there's no such thing as the paranormal ... only infinite varieties of normal we've yet to understand?

From acclaimed author Sol Luckman comes *Snooze*, the riveting tale of one extraordinary boy's awakening to the world-changing reality of his dreams, winner of the 2015 National Indie Excellence Award for New Age Fiction and 2016 Readers' Favorite International Book Award Finalist in the Young Adult-Coming of Age category.

Join Max Diver, aka "Snooze," along the razor's edge of a quest to rescue his astronaut father from a fate stranger than death in the exotic, perilous Otherworld of sleep.

An insightful look at a plethora of paranormal subjects, from Sasquatch and lucid dreaming to time travel via the Bermuda Triangle, *Snooze* also shines as a work of literature featuring iconic characters, intense drama and breathless pacing to stir you wide awake!

"Luckman's dazzling abilities as a novelist abound with lyrical prose ... If you enjoy colorful characters, a fast-paced plot and stories that tug at your heart, this novel in eighty-four chapters is anything but a yawn."
—Readers' Favorite

Snooze is "a multi-dimensional, many-faceted gem of a read. From mysteries to metaphysics, entering the dream world, Bigfoot, high magic and daring feats of courage, this book has it all."
—Lance White, author of *Tales of a Zany Mystic*

"*Snooze* is a book for readers ready to awaken from our mass cultural illusion before we self-destruct. *Snooze* calls out for readers open to the challenging adventure of opening their minds." —Merry Hall, Co-Host of *Envision This*

Learn more at **www.CrowRising.com**.

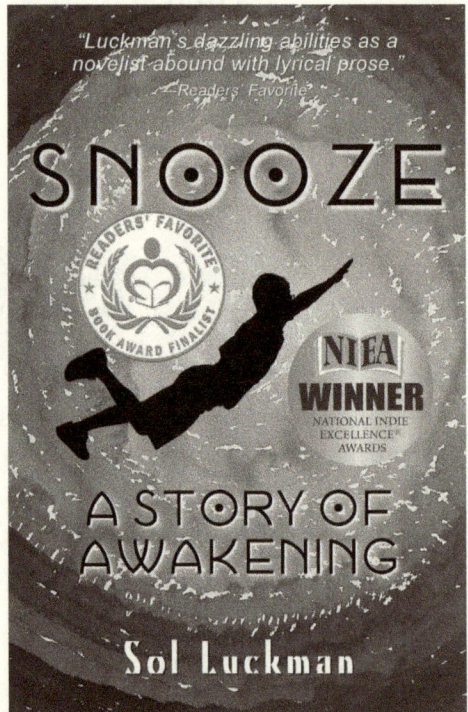

The first DNA activation in the "revolutionary healing science" (*Nexus*) of the Regenetics Method, Potentiation employs special linguistic codes—produced vocally and mentally—to stimulate a self-healing and transformational ability in DNA.

In this masterful exploration of sound healing by bestselling author Sol Luckman, learn how to activate your genetic potential—in a single, thirty-minute session!

Besides teaching you a leading-edge technique you can perform for your family, friends and even pets, *Potentiate Your DNA* also:

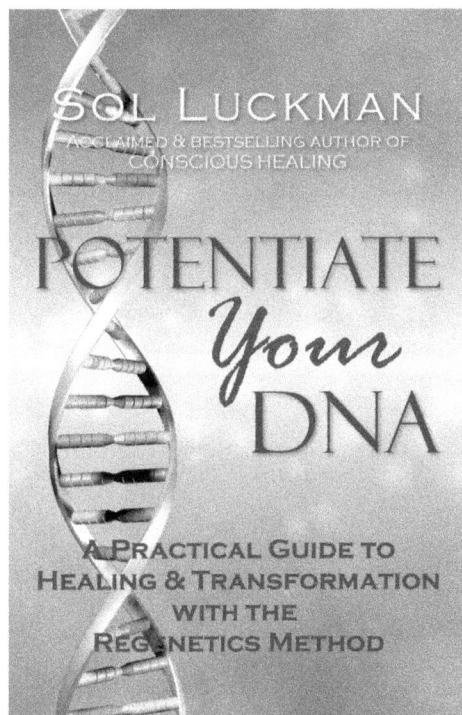

1. Provides a wealth of tried and true supplemental tools for maximizing your results; and

2. Outlines a pioneering theory linking genetics, energy and consciousness that is sure to inspire alternative and traditional healers alike.

Potentiate Your DNA "is both fascinating and an astounding, perhaps even world-changing theory." —*New Dawn* Magazine

"*Potentiate Your DNA* is brilliant and cutting-edge. Luckman has succinctly and elegantly provided a comprehensible intellectual framework for understanding the profound role of DNA in healing and transformation."
—Brendan D. Murphy, author of *The Grand Illusion*

"If you love the cutting-edge of the cutting-edge ... read this book!"
—Dr. David Kamnitzer

"The work defined in this book and Sol Luckman's previous book, *Conscious Healing*, should be the starting place of every health practice."
—Dr. Julie TwoMoon

Learn more at **www.PhoenixRegenetics.org**.

www.ingramcontent.com/pod-product-compliance
Lightning Source LLC
Chambersburg PA
CBHW031957080426
42735CB00007B/431